Original title:
Inner Harmony

Copyright © 2024 Creative Arts Management OÜ
All rights reserved.

Author: Thor Castlebury
ISBN HARDBACK: 978-9916-88-596-3
ISBN PAPERBACK: 978-9916-88-597-0

Navigate the Inner Waters

In silence deep, where shadows play,
I drift along the hidden way.
Beneath the calm, the currents flow,
Whispers of truth in undertow.

Each thought a raft, I gently steer,
Through waves of doubt, through strands of fear.
With every breath, new depths unfold,
A story long and still untold.

Reflections dance on waters clear,
Illuminating paths so near.
In stillness lies the way to find,
The compass forged by heart and mind.

So navigate with heart and grace,
Embrace the quiet, find your place.
For in those depths, wisdom waits,
To lead you home through open gates.

Celestial Embrace

Stars entwined in night's warm glow,
Whispered secrets, soft and low.
Dreams take flight on silver beams,
Hearts awakened, born of dreams.

Heaven's canvas paints the sky,
Galaxies in sweet reply.
In the dance of cosmic flight,
We find solace in the light.

A Harmony of Colors

In the garden, hues align,
Nature's brush strokes, pure divine.
Petals flutter, soft and bright,
Creating beauty, pure delight.

Amidst the dance of sun and shade,
Melodies of colors made.
With each hue, a story told,
Of love eternal, pure as gold.

Voices of the Inner Realm

Silent whispers, thoughts collide,
In the depths, we must confide.
Echoes linger, calling clear,
Listen closely, draw them near.

In the shadows, fears reside,
Yet within, we must abide.
With each voice, we start to mend,
Finding strength that won't descend.

Tides of Tranquility

Gentle waves caress the shore,
Time stands still, forevermore.
Moonlit paths on waters gleam,
Hearts embrace in tranquil dream.

Whispers of the ocean's sigh,
Breathe in peace, let troubles fly.
In this flow, we find our grace,
Eternal calm, a warm embrace.

The Light Between Shadows

In twilight's hush, the whispers glide,
A flicker caught where secrets hide.
Soft glimmers dance on edges near,
The heart looks out, the world appears.

From darkened corners, hope takes flight,
Revealing dreams that spark the night.
In shadows deep, we find our way,
Through fractured beams of breaking day.

Blooming in Silence

Among the roots where stillness breathes,
Petals unfold, a gentle tease.
With every pulse, the earth's embrace,
A quiet bloom, a sacred space.

In fragrant dusk, the whispers play,
Colors rise in soft ballet.
Each moment lingers, time unspools,
Nature sings in silent pools.

The Stillness of Being

In endless pauses, life unfolds,
A treasure trove of tales untold.
Each heartbeat echoes, calm and clear,
In stillness found, the soul draws near.

The tranquil breath of morning light,
Offers peace both deep and bright.
In every sigh, in every glance,
The world reveals its timeless dance.

A Journey to the Center

Through winding paths, our spirits roam,
Seeking the core, a place called home.
With every step, the layers shed,
To find the truth that dwells ahead.

In echoes lost, the lessons rise,
Maps drawn in starlit skies.
The center holds the stories vast,
A journey's end, a love steadfast.

In the Still Waters

In still waters, dreams reside,
Reflections whisper, night and tide.
Moonlight dances on the deep,
Secrets linger, shadows keep.

Softly gliding, time stands still,
Nature's calm, the heart to fill.
Ripples whisper tales untold,
In quiet depths, the soul unfolds.

Within the hush, a world unfolds,
Gentle stories, heartbeats bold.
Stars above in velvet sky,
Cradled by the night's sigh.

Each moment drifts, a fleeting glance,
In the silence, we find our chance.
To breathe, to feel, to simply be,
In still waters, we find free.

The Unseen Accord

In the silence, hearts align,
A rhythm found, a bond divine.
Unseen forces, pulsing near,
Together woven, crystal clear.

Through whispered winds and rustling leaves,
A subtle dance, the spirit weaves.
In the shadows, truths emerge,
Barely spoken, yet they surge.

Hand in hand, we walk this thread,
Guided by what's left unsaid.
In every glance, a silent pact,
Unity, in love intact.

In the twilight, dreams take flight,
Bound together, day to night.
The unseen accord, forever strong,
In our hearts, we each belong.

Nature's Gentle Song

Nature sings in softest tones,
Whispers carried by the stones.
Through the meadows, voices flow,
In each bloom, the symphony grows.

Birds are chirping, skies awake,
Every ripple, grace they make.
In the breeze, a lullaby,
Filling hearts as time drifts by.

The rustling trees and babbling brooks,
Crafting rhythm in nature's books.
Fluttering leaves, a dance of light,
Nature's song, a pure delight.

With every dawn, a fresh refrain,
Harmonies that wash our pain.
Nature's gentle song we hear,
A melody that draws us near.

A Tapestry of Calm

Threads of gold and shades of green,
Woven tightly, peace unseen.
In the quiet, worlds collide,
A tapestry where hearts reside.

Each color speaks, a silent shout,
In harmony, we weave about.
Intertwined, our stories blend,
A fabric rich that has no end.

In the stillness, patterns flow,
A dance of life, soft and slow.
Moments captured, time embraced,
In this calm, we find our place.

Stitching dreams with tender hands,
Creating warmth, as love expands.
A tapestry of calm and grace,
In unity, we find our space.

The Heart's Quiet Soliloquy

In the stillness of the night,
Whispers dance around my heart,
Echoes of forgotten dreams,
In shadows, memories depart.

Softly speaks the beating pulse,
Carving secrets in the dark,
Each rhythm a tale retold,
A flame igniting the spark.

In silence, love's essence blooms,
Gentle, yet profound and bright,
In the heart's quiet soliloquy,
Truth awakens in the light.

Echoing Silence of the Mind

In the chambers of the mind,
Thoughts weave patterns, strong yet frail,
Like autumn leaves in shifting winds,
They flutter, dance, and then they pale.

A void that speaks with lingering sounds,
Where shadows of the past reside,
In echoes, clarity appears,
In silence, visions often hide.

The whispers of a restless breeze,
Stir doubts and dreams in hushed retreat,
Yet from this quiet, wisdom grows,
In stillness, our heartbeats meet.

The Unfolding Essence of Being

Life's petals open one by one,
In dawn's embrace, they stretch and yearn,
Each moment holds a mystery,
In the light, our spirits burn.

The essence flows like rivers wide,
Nourishing every weary soul,
In countless forms, it weaves and bends,
A tapestry that makes us whole.

In laughter's echo, sorrow's sigh,
An endless cycle, ebb and flow,
Through every joy, each tear we shed,
The essence of being starts to grow.

Whispers of the Soul

Deep within, a soft refrain,
A melody of untold grace,
In whispers carried by the wind,
The soul finds its steadfast place.

Thoughts like feathers drift and fall,
Each one a note in life's grand score,
In harmony, we learn to dance,
Embracing all that came before.

With every breath, a story breathes,
In stillness, wisdom starts to unfold,
The whispers of the soul ignite,
A flame of truth, brave and bold.

Whispers of Tranquil Souls

In the stillness of dusk's embrace,
Gentle breezes find their place.
Stars awaken, softly gleam,
Carrying whispers, like a dream.

Moonlight glistens on the lake,
Silent ripples, hearts awake.
Peaceful thoughts in quiet flow,
Nature's voice begins to grow.

Trees sway lightly, roots hold tight,
In the calm of the night.
Every shadow tells a tale,
In this tranquil world, we sail.

Together in the gentle night,
Finding solace in the light.
Whispers linger, as we drift,
In the stillness, our souls lift.

Echoes of Serene Hearts

Beneath the arch of endless skies,
Softly whispering lullabies.
Leaves flutter with a tender grace,
In this gathering, we find our place.

Rippling streams hum sweet refrain,
Echoes of joy, a soft domain.
Hearts entwined in nature's song,
In serene moments, we belong.

Clouds drift slowly, dreams take flight,
Painting visions in soft light.
In the silence, fears depart,
Echoes linger, healing heart.

Through every breath, we feel alive,
In this harmony, we thrive.
Serenity in all we share,
Echoes of love are everywhere.

The Dance of Quietude

In the hush of morning's grace,
Hope and calm find their space.
Gentle whispers in the breeze,
Filling hearts with tranquil ease.

A soft ballet of nature's art,
Each moment plays a vital part.
Clouds drift slowly, curtains drawn,
On this canvas, we are reborn.

Stars twirl in the velvet night,
Guiding souls with their soft light.
Harmony in every beat,
In this dance, we find our seat.

Together, moving, side by side,
In the quiet, hearts confide.
As nightfall yields to dawn's embrace,
We dance in time, our sacred space.

Mosaics of Stillness

A tapestry of quiet grace,
Each moment finds its rightful place.
Colors blend in soft delight,
Mosaics shimmer in the light.

In the stillness, peace unfolds,
Nature's stories softly told.
Fragments of a tranquil past,
In this moment, our hearts hold fast.

Gentle waves kiss the shore,
A soothing rhythm, wanting more.
Each heartbeat tells a tale anew,
Mosaics paint the world in hue.

Embracing silence, we unite,
Finding beauty in the night.
In the stillness, we are free,
Mosaics of our history.

Melodies of Peaceful Reflections

Whispers of calm in gentle waves,
Echoes of thoughts, where the heart braves.
Softly they dance, these moments bright,
Guiding us through the deep of night.

A symphony hums in the silent air,
Each note a story, tender and rare.
In the stillness, we find our way,
Melodies woven with dreams that stay.

Clouds drift slowly across the sky,
Painting the canvas where hopes lie.
Every reflection, a fleeting glance,
In the depth of quiet, we find our chance.

Through shadows cast by the setting sun,
The journey unfolds, never to shun.
In the embrace of tranquil streams,
We write our tales, weaving sweet dreams.

The Light in Silent Spaces

Amidst the hush, a soft glow gleams,
Illuminating all our dreams.
In silence deep, the heart can see,
A light that whispers, "Set yourself free."

Beneath the stars, where shadows fade,
Hope flickers gently, unafraid.
In the quiet, wisdom grows,
A guiding star in stillness shows.

Every heartbeat sings a prayer,
In the silence, love lays bare.
Light dances softly on the skin,
Inviting peace to dwell within.

In the corners where echoes cease,
Lies the strength of inner peace.
A sanctuary of boundless grace,
The soul awakens in this space.

Unveiling the Hidden Stillness

In the depths where silence lies,
Lies a treasure in disguise.
Layers peeled, like petals unwind,
Reveal the calm that hearts can find.

Ceaseless moments whisper low,
Time flows gently, like a slow glow.
With every breath, the stillness grows,
A sacred trust that softly knows.

Waves of thought drift and sway,
In quietude, they find their way.
Hidden truths begin to rise,
When we listen with open eyes.

Within the pause, the world is whole,
A gentle balm upon the soul.
Unveiling peace, we come to see,
The beauty held in reverie.

Tides of Self-Discovery

Upon the shore where waves embrace,
We find the rhythm, we find our place.
Tides that ebb, and tides that flow,
Guide us inward, where we grow.

In every shell, a story lies,
Echoing whispers, ancient cries.
Embrace the mystery, let it teach,
The lessons only tides can reach.

As footprints wash away from sand,
New paths appear, unplanned and grand.
In the dance of water's grace,
We find the strength to leave our trace.

Through the tides, we come alive,
In the current, we will thrive.
A journey deep, like ocean's art,
Self-discovery, a beating heart.

Softly Unraveling

Threads of light in gentle sway,
A tapestry of night and day.
The breeze whispers secrets near,
Softly unraveling hearts sincere.

Moonlit dreams that fade away,
Hopes entwined in soft ballet.
Each shadow holds a silent tear,
Softly unraveling, we draw near.

Stars above, like thoughts unspooled,
Moments cherished, never fooled.
In the quiet, fears disappear,
Softly unraveling, love is here.

Embrace the calm, let go of strife,
In every fold, the dance of life.
We breathe the peace, our spirits leer,
Softly unraveling, season clear.

Lost in Quietude

In gentle laps of silver tide,
I hear the whispers, feel the ride.
Moments linger, soft and slow,
Lost in quietude, time will flow.

A world asleep beneath the stars,
Worries fade, forgotten scars.
The heart speaks softly, without pride,
Lost in quietude, dreams abide.

Nature hums a lulling song,
In this stillness, we belong.
Every gaze a soothing guide,
Lost in quietude, hearts collide.

With every breath, the stress dissolves,
In tranquil depths, our souls revolve.
Embrace the peace, let the world bide,
Lost in quietude, worlds beside.

Echoing Whispers of the Heart

In the stillness, soft and low,
Whispers echo, feelings flow.
Tender secrets gently part,
Echoing whispers of the heart.

Every sigh a story tells,
In silence, love's magic dwells.
The pulse of dreams, like sacred art,
Echoing whispers, deep and smart.

Moments held in tender grace,
Time suspended, a sweet embrace.
The melody of souls impart,
Echoing whispers, never depart.

In the dusk, as shadows start,
Hope ignites, a brand new chart.
Feel the rhythm, play your part,
Echoing whispers of the heart.

The Calm Canvas

Upon the stillness, colors blend,
A tranquil portrait, dreams extend.
Brush strokes dance with gentle grace,
The calm canvas holds our space.

Hues of peace in soft embrace,
Layered whispers, time can trace.
Every shade, a story penned,
The calm canvas knows no end.

In the light, reflections play,
Creating worlds where we can stay.
Each heartbeat paints a steadfast face,
The calm canvas, our resting place.

Emotions flow in vibrant streams,
Art of life, woven dreams.
With every breath, our hopes advance,
The calm canvas, a timeless dance.

Caress of the Gentle Breeze

Whispers float through evening air,
As leaves sway with a quiet grace.
The sun dips low, a tender flare,
Nature's touch, a warm embrace.

Gentle kisses brush the skin,
Each sigh a promise softly shared.
In this moment, peace begins,
A world where every heart is bared.

The meadow hums a soothing tune,
While shadows dance beneath the trees.
Underneath the silver moon,
Life glides on the gentle breeze.

In twilight's glow, dreams take flight,
Through the stillness, hope will find.
A reminder in the night,
That love and peace are intertwined.

Symphony of Soft Thoughts

In the silence of the night,
Whispers weave a melodic flow.
Ideas take their gentle flight,
In the mind, their colors glow.

Each notion dances, light as air,
A symphony of pure delight.
Floating softly without a care,
As dreams awaken with the light.

A harmony of hearts entwined,
In quiet corners, musings bloom.
Soft thoughts linger, sweetly aligned,
Filling the soul with fragrant perfume.

A chorus of love, a gentle peace,
Lifting spirits, setting free.
In this moment, life's sweet release,
Together, we find our harmony.

The Calm Within Chaos

Amid the storm, the heart beats still,
A quiet space in reckless roar.
Finding peace against the will,
Moments lost, yet so much more.

Chaos whispers, shadows play,
Yet in the eye, calmness reigns.
Finding light in disarray,
Hope persists, despite the chains.

In rumbles deep, a silent grin,
Resilience forged in swirling strife.
From raging waves, we rise within,
A testament to love and life.

Through thunder's cry, we stay composed,
An anchor in the tempest's path.
Together, we shall face what's opposed,
The calm within all that we hath.

Garden of Blended Dreams

In a garden where hopes meet,
Petals bloom in vivid hues.
Each flower tells a tale so sweet,
A dance of choice, a path we choose.

Beneath the sky, the stars unite,
In twilight's glow, we find our way.
Dreams mingle softly through the night,
Creating dawn from shadows gray.

A tapestry of wishes shared,
With gentle hands, we plant the seeds.
In every heart, a love declared,
Nurtured deep, fulfilling needs.

Together we shall walk this lane,
Through seasons bright and trials bleak.
In this garden, joy and pain,
A sanctuary for the meek.

Unbroken Whispers

In the hush of night,
Soft echoes find their way,
Gentle secrets intertwine,
Whispers dance and sway.

Stars weave tales above,
Each twinkle a soft sigh,
Hints of love and longing,
Carried through the sky.

Beneath the moonlit glow,
Hearts are free to roam,
In the warmth of silence,
We find a place called home.

Unbroken are these ties,
Across the vast expanse,
In whispers, we unite,
In the dark, we dance.

Confluence of Thoughts

Streams of reason merge,
Ideas swirl and flow,
In the quiet moments,
New pathways start to grow.

Minds connect like rivers,
Flowing into one,
In the depth of silence,
Countless dreams begun.

Understanding blossoms,
Like flowers in the sun,
Together we create,
As we become as one.

In this boundless tether,
Our hearts ignite the spark,
A confluence of thoughts,
Illuminates the dark.

Serenity's Embrace

A soft, gentle breeze,
Whispers through the trees,
In the calm of twilight,
All worries set at ease.

The ocean's lullaby,
Cradles the weary soul,
In serenity's arms,
We discover we are whole.

Stars twinkle like dreams,
Guiding us from afar,
In the night's embrace,
We find who we are.

Beneath the quiet skies,
Peace settles like a sigh,
In the stillness of night,
Our spirits learn to fly.

The Gentle Path of Being

With each step we take,
A journey unfolds wide,
The gentle path of being,
Where love and hope reside.

In the rustling leaves,
Whispers of the ground,
Nature's voice reminds us,
Life's magic can be found.

Colors brush the sky,
With lessons in each hue,
In every moment lived,
A chance to start anew.

Through valleys and peaks,
In stillness we shall stand,
The gentle path awaits,
With an open hand.

Guided by the Heart

In shadows deep, where feelings dwell,
A whisper soft, a silent spell.
The pulse of love, a gentle guide,
In every tear, the truth abides.

With open arms, we dare to dream,
Embracing warmth, like sunlit beam.
Our spirits dance, entwined as one,
A journey bright, beneath the sun.

Each step we take, in tender grace,
A rhythm found, in time and space.
With courage strong, we face the night,
Guided by the heart's pure light.

In echoes sweet, our laughter sings,
A tapestry of simple things.
Through trials faced, our bonds will grow,
Together tread, where love will flow.

Melodies of the Mind

A symphony within the heart,
Each thought a note, each dream a part.
In quiet minds, the echoes swell,
Whispers of wisdom, tales to tell.

The laughter blooms in playful tunes,
As moonlight casts on midnight dunes.
In harmony, we find our way,
A dance of minds, come what may.

Boundless dreams take wing and soar,
In creative realms, we explore.
With every beat, a world unfolds,
In melodies, our truth beholds.

Let passions rise, let feelings flow,
A canvas vast where visions glow.
In symphonic hues, we discover,
The magic found in each other.

The Serenity Spectrum

In hues of calm, the world unfolds,
A tranquil scene, its beauty molds.
With gentle waves, the oceans play,
A symphony of peace each day.

Through life's embrace, we wander wide,
In nature's arms, where dreams abide.
Each moment holds a whispered grace,
In stillness found, we find our place.

As silver stars wink in the night,
The heart finds solace, pure delight.
In every breath, serenity grows,
A spectrum wide, where beauty flows.

Let worries fade, like mist at dawn,
In quietude, our spirits drawn.
With open hearts, the journey starts,
In harmony, we join all hearts.

Interludes of Joy

A sparkle bright in laughter's wake,
Each fleeting moment, joy we stake.
In playful jests, our spirits rise,
With every giggle, we touch the skies.

Through winding paths of light we dance,
In serendipity, we find our chance.
With arms outstretched, we'll spin and twirl,
Embracing bliss in every swirl.

In simple things, the magic flows,
Like fragrant blooms in springtime shows.
A shared glance speaks, a bond so dear,
In every heartbeat, joy draws near.

So let us chase the sunshine's grace,
In laughter's arms, we find our place.
Together weave the threads of cheer,
In interludes of joy sincere.

Inward Journeys

In shadows deep, I wander slow,
Through paths of thought where whispers flow.
Each step unfolds a hidden trail,
A secret world where dreams set sail.

The echoes dance in silence bright,
Illuminating the inner light.
Reflections spark with each new breath,
A canvas brushed 'twixt life and death.

I find my peace in quiet gaze,
As time and space begin to glaze.
With every thought, a new refrain,
Inward journeys through joy and pain.

The heart's soft beat, a guiding song,
In this deep well, I feel I belong.
Each moment treasured, a stitch of grace,
Inward journeys, my sacred space.

The Still Life of Thought

A still life blooms in quiet mind,
Where colors blend and shapes unwind.
The shadows play upon the wall,
In tranquil whispers, I hear their call.

Brush strokes of dreams, a palette wide,
In moments paused, where visions bide.
Captured echoes of soft delight,
In the still life, I find my flight.

The gentle sway of timeless grace,
Frames the beauty of this space.
Each thought a petal, gently laid,
In the still life, I'm unafraid.

A canvas stretched with thoughts so rare,
A masterpiece beyond compare.
In every breath, I come alive,
In the still life, my spirit thrives.

Dreaming in Quietude

In softest folds of night I drift,
Where silence weaves a peaceful gift.
Dreaming beneath the starry dome,
In quietude, I find my home.

Phantom visions dance in air,
Whispers of moments bold and rare.
Each sigh a note in twilight's tune,
Dreaming gently beneath the moon.

The world outside a distant sigh,
In quietude, I learn to fly.
Each thought a feather, light and free,
In dreams, I glimpse eternity.

As dawn breaks cool, the dreams subside,
Yet in my heart, they still reside.
In quietude, I'll seek and find,
The hidden wonders of the mind.

Serenity's Guest

A gentle breeze through open space,
The warmth of sun, a soft embrace.
As moments linger, slow and vast,
I welcome peace, my shadows cast.

Serenity kneels beside my soul,
In soothing tones, it makes me whole.
With every breath, a calm descends,
In quiet moments, the heart mends.

The world's loud clamor dims away,
In tranquil folds, I choose to stay.
Embracing stillness, I find the way,
As serenity's guest, I long to play.

So let the hours softly flow,
With every pulse, a chance to grow.
In peace, I dance, a gentle zest,
Forever bound as serenity's guest.

Embrace of the Whispering Mind

In shadows where thoughts softly play,
Whispers dance like leaves in May.
A gentle touch upon the shore,
Echoes beckon, asking for more.

Secrets wrapped in silent sighs,
A world unseen, where wisdom lies.
With every breath, a story unfolds,
In the embrace of the mind, truths are told.

Moments linger, tender and light,
Holding dreams that take to flight.
In quiet corners, peace is found,
Where the whispers of the soul resound.

Together we float on a river of thought,
In the stillness, we find what's sought.
Embraced by the whispers, soft and kind,
We journey deep into the mind.

The Balance Weaving Through Time

In the tapestry of dusk and dawn,
Threads of life are quietly drawn.
Moments collide in a graceful ballet,
Painting the hours in shades of gray.

We walk the line of ebb and flow,
Finding the beauty in what we sow.
Each choice a stitch, each tear a sign,
In the rhythm, we discover the divine.

Winds of change carry tales untold,
In whispers of silver and threads of gold.
With every heartbeat, our stories chime,
In the balance, we dance through time.

Connections made, and laughter shared,
In quiet moments, hearts are bared.
As we navigate the paths we climb,
We become the balance weaving through time.

Reflections in the Mirror of Solitude

In the stillness, shadows rise,
Mirrored truths in unseen skies.
Echoes whisper of dreams long past,
In silence, our voices at last.

The heart unfolds in quiet embrace,
Finding solace in inner space.
With every glance, the soul ignites,
In solitude's calm, the spirit lights.

Fragments of self come into view,
In reflections, we learn what's true.
Amidst the stillness, we dare to feel,
In the mirror, the wounds may heal.

A sanctuary built from whispers and sighs,
Here in the silence, the spirit flies.
Embraced in the quiet, we find our way,
In the mirror of solitude, we stay.

Harmonies of the Quiet Soul

Within the hush, the notes arise,
Singing softly beneath the skies.
Gentle chords weave through the night,
Filling the heart with pure delight.

Every whisper a soothing balm,
In the stillness, we find our calm.
Together we dance to the rhythm of peace,
In harmonies, our worries cease.

With each heartbeat, the melody flows,
Revealing the beauty that gently grows.
In the symphony of dreams untold,
The quiet soul, a treasure to hold.

In the serene, our spirits soar,
Embracing the music forevermore.
With harmonies wrapped in love's sweet goal,
We find our place: the quiet soul.

Alchemy of Peace

In the stillness of the night,
Whispers dance on the breeze.
Hearts unite in calm delight,
Bound by love, our souls at ease.

Gentle hands weave the thread,
Of hope that will not fray.
In silence, fears are shed,
Together we find our way.

With every breath, we create,
A world where kindness thrives.
In the warmth of shared fate,
The alchemy of our lives.

Harmony plays its song,
Through valleys deep and wide.
In peace, we all belong,
As hearts and spirits glide.

Woven Threads of Serenity

In the tapestry of time,
Colors blend and entwine.
Each thread a silent rhyme,
In harmony, we shine.

Moments stitched with laughter,
Peaceful patterns unfold.
Crafting dreams ever after,
In warmth, we break the cold.

Softly in twilight's glow,
We gather, hand in hand.
With whispers of the flow,
Together, we take a stand.

Woven stories softly told,
In fabric, love is sewn.
In the quiet, bold and bold,
Serenity has grown.

Radiance of the Spirit

In the dawn's first light,
We awaken to the day.
A spark ignites our sight,
As shadows fade away.

Each heartbeat, a drum's call,
Energizing the soul.
In unity, we enthrall,
Together, we are whole.

Laughter's echoing tune,
Calls forth the vibrant dance.
We shine beneath the moon,
In joy, we find our chance.

Radiance fills the air,
In every loving glance.
We rise beyond despair,
In gratitude's expanse.

Moonlight Meditation

Under the silver glow,
We find a peaceful space.
The tranquil waters flow,
Reflecting calm embrace.

In silence, spirits soar,
Beneath the stars so bright.
Through whispers, we explore,
The depths of endless night.

Each moment feels so pure,
As dreams begin to blend.
With thoughts that gently lure,
To where our hearts extend.

Moonlight's soothing song,
Wraps us in soft delight.
In this dance, we belong,
As shadows take their flight.

A Resilient Stillness

In whispers soft, the night draws near,
The world slows down, as dreams appear.
Beneath the moon, the shadows play,
A balm for hearts, a hushed ballet.

Amidst the storms that life may send,
A tranquil heart learns how to mend.
With every breath, a strength we find,
In stillness, we embrace our mind.

The chaos fades, the silence blooms,
In quietude, there's room for rooms.
We dance with fear, we learn the art,
Of finding peace within the heart.

So let the world spin wild and fast,
In stillness, we can make it last.
A quiet strength, a gentle grace,
A resilient stillness, our embrace.

Chasing the Golden Hour

The sun dips low, painting the sky,
A canvas wrought with hues of fire.
We chase the glow, the fleeting light,
In whispered dreams of day and night.

With every step, the shadows grow,
In warm embrace, we find our glow.
The golden hour, a fleeting dance,
Inviting souls to take a chance.

As time unravels like a thread,
Moments linger in what's said.
A tapestry of light and shade,
In nature's arms, our hearts parade.

On paths unknown, our spirits soar,
Chasing the light, we seek for more.
In every sunset, hope is found,
A fleeting magic all around.

The Rhythm of Reflection

In still waters, the mind takes flight,
Searching depths of shadowed light.
Thoughts ripple out, then merge and blend,
In quiet pools, new paths we send.

Each moment holds a whispered truth,
A dance of wisdom from our youth.
The ebb and flow, a timeless tune,
In solitude, we dare commune.

With every glance, our past unfolds,
Stories whispered, tenderly told.
The rhythm beats within the soul,
In reflection's arms, we feel whole.

So pause awhile, let silence reign,
In the depths, embrace joy and pain.
The heart knows paths that eyes can't see,
In reflection's gaze, we find the key.

Pilgrimage to Peace

On winding roads, our journey starts,
A quest that flows through open hearts.
With every step, the burdens fade,
In search of calm, our fears allayed.

Through valleys deep and mountains high,
We wander forth beneath the sky.
In nature's arms, we shed the weight,
A pilgrimage that sings of fate.

With every breath, a prayer is said,
To find the light where hope has led.
In every moment, peace draws near,
A solace found within our fear.

As stars emerge to guide the way,
In quiet nights, we learn to stay.
The pilgrimage, a sacred art,
A journey crafted in the heart.

The Breath Between Moments

In silence, whispers softly dwell,
The heartbeat of a fleeting spell.
An instant caught, a fleeting glance,
Life held still in quiet dance.

A pause that holds the world's embrace,
Where time can slow, a gentle pace.
Like dew upon the morning grass,
These breaths we take, too sweet to pass.

Each moment speaks, yet few will hear,
The subtle truth that draws us near.
In every sigh, a story told,
Of dreams unfurled and moments bold.

So cherish well the breaths we share,
In stillness find what's truly rare.
For in the pause, our hearts align,
In breath between, our souls entwine.

Radiance of the Resilient Spirit

Through storms that howl and shadows creep,
A light persists beneath the deep.
With every trial, the heart stands tall,
A beacon bright through it all.

In ashes cold, the embers glow,
From pain, the strength begins to grow.
Each wound a mark, each scar a sign,
Of battles fought, a life divine.

Resilience flows through veins of gold,
A story rich that must be told.
With every sunrise comes the fight,
To rise again, to claim the light.

So let us celebrate the brave,
The spirits bold who learn to wave.
For every challenge faced with grace,
Is proof of love, our warm embrace.

Still Waters Run Deep

In tranquil pools, reflections sway,
Beneath the calm, the depths at play.
What stirs below may yet surprise,
The secrets held from prying eyes.

Like silent dreams that softly flow,
In depths of thought, we seldom know.
Emotions swirl beneath the crust,
In quietude, our minds adjust.

For peace is found in gentle streams,
Where solitude cradles our dreams.
With every ripple, stories rise,
Whispered softly through muted sighs.

So pause awhile and dare to dive,
Into the depths where thoughts contrive.
In stillness, truths begin to gleam,
And hearts are healed through hope's sweet dream.

A Canvas of Gentle Colors

In twilight hues that softly blend,
A palette rich, where moments send.
Brushstrokes dance upon the sky,
As day gives way, the night draws nigh.

Each color tells a tale profound,
Of laughter lost and love unbound.
From dusky pinks to deepened blues,
A tapestry of varied views.

The canvas holds our joys and fears,
In gentle strokes, the laughter cheers.
With every dawn, new shades appear,
A vibrant world, refreshed and clear.

So may we paint with heart and soul,
In every hue, find ways to console.
For life's a canvas, vast and wide,
In colors bright, let dreams reside.

When Light Meets Shadow

In the dance of dusk and dawn,
Light whispers secrets, shadows yawn.
Colors blend in a gentle sigh,
As day fades out, the stars will fly.

Soft beams touch the darkened ground,
In this silence, peace is found.
Each flicker blends, a sweet embrace,
As night falls in its velvet grace.

Echoes of warmth in the cool night air,
A tender moment, spirits aware.
Where light retreats and shadows play,
A world transformed, as night meets day.

The balance held, a fragile thread,
A waltz of life where none dare tread.
In the mingling of dark and bright,
We find our truth in the still of night.

The Soul's Resonance

Whispers of the heart's deep song,
Echos of where we all belong.
In every breath, a gentle plea,
The soul reaches out, seeking to be free.

Melodies rise from shadows cast,
In harmony, the die is cast.
In every note, a story shared,
A journey felt, though none prepared.

In silence, we find connection true,
The pulse of life flows, always new.
Each rhythm lifts us, takes us higher,
Igniting within, a vibrant fire.

Beneath the noise, a tender thread,
Binding our paths, souls gently led.
In the resonance, find your place,
Embrace the music, the endless grace.

Everlasting Ascent

With each step, the mountains call,
A journey rising, I will not fall.
Through valleys low and skies so wide,
The spirit strengthens, my heart my guide.

In the chill of dawn's first light,
Hope ignites, dispelling night.
With every breath, the summit near,
The peaks await, hold no fear.

Stars above like distant dreams,
Whisper tales and ancient themes.
A climber's heart, both bold and free,
Adventures born from what will be.

As aspen leaves in softest breeze,
I soar on winds, my soul at ease.
With every climb, I reach for more,
In everlasting ascent, I soar.

Beneath the Surface

Ripples dance on the water's edge,
Secrets linger where shadows hedge.
Depths conceal what eyes can't see,
A world alive, a mystery.

The moonlight kisses the tranquil sea,
In silence, whispers call to me.
Bubbles rise with stories untold,
Of treasures found, of dreams so bold.

In the stillness, wonders dwell,
In amber depths, a hidden spell.
Life emerges from darkened space,
Beneath the surface, a warm embrace.

In every dive, heartbeats blend,
Where journeys start and never end.
Embrace the depths, let go the fear,
For beneath the surface, love is near.

The Art of Listening Within

In silence, I find my truth,
Each whisper of my heart,
A gentle guide through the shadows,
Where shadows play their part.

With every breath, a story shared,
Echoes of wisdom, soft and near,
The art of listening blooms within,
In stillness, I quietly hear.

I tune into the whispers deep,
Where dreams and fears entwine,
With open heart, I slowly seek,
The treasures that are mine.

A dance of thoughts, a melody,
In the quiet of my soul,
Listening within, I find the key,
To be truly whole.

Mosaic of Contentment

Fragments of joy, moments bright,
Colors blend in the light,
Each piece a part of my story,
A tapestry of delight.

In the quiet whispering hours,
I gather the shards of my day,
Crafting a mosaic of content,
In shades of gentle gray.

Every smile and every tear,
In this patchwork, they belong,
Together they weave a portrait,
In perfect shades of song.

Finding beauty in the scattered,
In life's chaotic dance,
I embrace each tiny fragment,
In the mosaic, I find my chance.

The Calm Before the Storm

A hush blankets the world outside,
As shadows stretch and sigh,
The air is thick with longing,
Beneath the brooding sky.

Birds retreat, their songs subdued,
Winds whisper tales untold,
Nature holds her breath in wait,
As the gray begins to fold.

The horizon dances, swirling,
A tempest starts to brew,
Yet in the stillness, hope abides,
As crows take to the blue.

I stand in this fragile moment,
A canvas rich and warm,
Aware that beauty leans on dread,
In the calm before the storm.

Harmonious Echoes

A symphony in every breath,
Notes of life intertwine,
Each heartbeat, a gentle pulse,
In rhythm, we align.

The rustling leaves, a melody,
The rivers sing their song,
Harmonious echoes all around,
Reminding us we belong.

In laughter shared, in gentle touch,
In silence, our hearts meet,
The world spins on, a bright ballet,
In unity, we greet.

Together in this grand design,
Where every voice is free,
We weave the threads of life's refrain,
In harmonious melody.

Serene Reflections

In the stillness of dawn, soft hues bloom,
Gentle whispers of light dispel the gloom.
Mirrors of water, a tranquil embrace,
Nature's canvas painted with grace.

Mountains rise high, guarding the peace,
Where thoughts dance freely, and worries cease.
Underneath stars, the world feels right,
In serene reflections, hearts take flight.

Ripples of calm through the chilling breeze,
Echoes of moments put hearts at ease.
Time stands still, as we breathe in deep,
In the serene reflections, our souls we keep.

With every sigh, a story unfolds,
Of dreams and journeys yet to be told.
In the quiet embrace of soft twilight,
Serene reflections bring pure delight.

Embrace of the Mind

Thoughts intertwine like vines on a wall,
Each whispering secret, a delicate call.
In shadows and light, the echoes reside,
In the embrace of the mind, we confide.

Moments of stillness, a soft retreat,
Where memories linger, and dreams compete.
Like a gentle breeze through fields so wide,
In the embrace of the mind, we abide.

Waves of creation, a tempest inside,
In the maze of thoughts where fears can hide.
Finding the path to our heart's design,
In the embrace of the mind, we align.

Through tempest and calm, our spirits soar,
With every new challenge, we grow more sure.
Reflecting on treasures that time can't bind,
Lost in the labyrinth, yet we find.

Colors of wisdom in shadows and light,
Guiding our steps through the dark of the night.
In the embrace of the mind, we seek truth,
Awakening dreams from the depths of our youth.

Harmony in the Silence

In silence profound, the soul can hear,
A symphony playing, soft and clear.
Notes of the heart in gentle refrain,
In harmony found, we release the pain.

Nature's quiet hum, a blissful song,
Whispers of wisdom where we belong.
Every heartbeat a note, strong and true,
In harmony's grace, we start anew.

Colors of dusk paint the world so bright,
Stars like diamonds ignite the night.
In the stillness, our spirits align,
Finding the joy in the peace we find.

Embracing stillness, like a calming sea,
Where every breath is a part of the key.
In harmony's arms, we learn to be,
Connected to all, forever free.

The Quietude Journey

Beneath the starlit sky, we wander slow,
Finding the paths where gentle winds blow.
Each step a whisper, a tale to tell,
On the quietude journey, all is well.

A forest of dreams, where shadows play,
In the still of the night, fears fade away.
With every heartbeat, the world feels right,
The quietude journey, a dance of light.

Mountains of thought, we scale with ease,
Seeking a refuge in rustling leaves.
The journey unfolds in soft twilight,
Guided by starlight, our spirits take flight.

With open hearts, we embrace the unknown,
Bound by the essence, we're never alone.
In the quiet depth of each soul's song,
The quietude journey, where we belong.

Cascades of Calm

Gentle whispers in the breeze,
A dance of leaves upon the trees.
Softly flowing, nature's stream,
Bringing forth a tranquil dream.

Mountains stand with silent grace,
Reflecting peace in every space.
Clouds drift by, so light and free,
In this realm, I long to be.

Sunlight bathes the world in gold,
Crafting tales from days of old.
Each droplet sparkles, crystal clear,
A symphony for all to hear.

In the distance, echoes play,
Serenading the fleeting day.
In cascades, calmness reigns true,
Nature's gift, forever new.

Illumination of the Heart

Beneath the stars, the soul ignites,
Whispers of love, like soft moonlight.
Every heartbeat tells a tale,
Of journeys shared on love's sweet trail.

Glistening dreams, so pure, so bright,
Chasing shadows into the night.
With every glance, a promise made,
In love's embrace, we are unafraid.

Flickering flames, emotions rise,
Lighting paths under infinite skies.
Together we dance, a sacred art,
Guided by the illumination of the heart.

Through storms and trials, hand in hand,
In this life, together we stand.
Bound by trust, and freedom's call,
In love's soft glow, we find our all.

Echoes in the Quiet

Through the stillness, secrets sigh,
Hints of stories weaving nigh.
Moments linger, softly spun,
In whispers shared, two hearts become one.

The clock ticks slow, a gentle hum,
Past and future merging, all become.
In silence deep, voices appear,
Echoes of love, forever near.

Rustling leaves, the twilight song,
Reminding us where we belong.
In every pause, meanings collide,
Echoes in the quiet, our love's guide.

Stars twinkle softly in the night,
Filling the dark with silver light.
In this calm, we find our way,
Embracing echoes that softly say.

Threads of Balance

Weaving worlds from thoughts and dreams,
Each thread connects, or so it seems.
With every breath, we shape our fate,
Entangled lives, we navigate.

Harmony sings in every note,
In life's vast ocean, we float.
Finding rhythm, hatreds cease,
In every moment, seek your peace.

Light and shadow dance in time,
Balancing moments, sweet and sublime.
Through ups and downs, our spirits soar,
Together we can, strive for more.

Fragile threads, yet strong at heart,
In unity, we play our part.
In life's embrace, we shall enhance,
Finding joy in each circumstance.

Requiem for Raging Thoughts

In the tempest of my mind, they swirl,
Whispers of doubt, a chaotic whirl.
Fragments of fear crash like waves,
Yearning for calm, where silence saves.

Beneath the storm, a quiet plea,
Hope flickers gently, a soft decree.
To shatter the noise, I seek the light,
Embrace the shadows, release the fight.

With every breath, I weave a pause,
Creating stillness, a sacred cause.
Thoughts like feathers drift from me,
In the quiet, I start to see.

A requiem sung for those lost dreams,
Not in vain; they stitch new seams.
I bury the fury, let it rest,
In the silence, I find my quest.

The Flow of Centered Existence

In the river of time, I gently float,
Carried by currents, a humble boat.
Moments unfold like petals wide,
In the embrace of the changing tide.

Anchored in peace, my spirit breathes,
In the quiet dance of autumn leaves.
The chaos behind me, a distant hum,
In this tranquil flow, I am become.

Each heartbeat echoes a gentle sound,
A rhythm of life, serene and profound.
As waves kiss shores, I find my ground,
In the flow of existence, I am unbound.

With every inhale, I trace the vast,
The whispers of moments that have passed.
Centered in presence, I rise and fall,
In the flow of being, I hear the call.

Footprints in the Serene Sand

Walk with me along this tranquil shore,
Where whispers of waves tell tales of yore.
Footprints fade in the golden light,
Echoes of souls, lost in the night.

Each grain of sand, a moment past,
Stories woven, yet never to last.
In the silence, I hear their song,
A melody sweet, where we all belong.

With every step, I leave my trace,
Marking the earth with a gentle grace.
The tide draws close to erase the line,
Yet in my heart, those moments shine.

Like whispers of wind that guide my way,
I cherish the footprints, come what may.
In the serene sand, I find my peace,
In every rhythm, my worries cease.

The Gentle Art of Letting Go

In the garden of memories, I tend my soul,
Nurturing blooms that make me whole.
Yet the seasons shift, and petals fall,
A gentle reminder to heed the call.

In the rapture of holding, I grasp too tight,
Learning the dance of both shadow and light.
With open hands, I release the past,
Trusting that change brings beauty at last.

Each sigh like a wave upon the shore,
Teaching me patience, forevermore.
I gather the strength to set it free,
To embrace the ebb of life's vast sea.

The art of letting go brings peace anew,
A canvas of dreams, painted in hues.
In wave after wave, I find my flow,
In the gentle release, I learn to grow.

When Stillness Speaks

In quiet moments, whispers float,
The heart listens to what's not spoke.
Time lingers softly, peace surrounds,
As tranquil shadows dance without sounds.

A gentle breeze sways through the trees,
Nature's symphony, a tranquil tease.
In this embrace, worries dissolve,
In stillness, we find what we evolve.

Eyes closed tight, the world fades away,
In the hush, we let our souls sway.
Finding calm in the depths of the night,
When stillness speaks, our souls take flight.

In the Space Between

Between the heartbeats, magic lies,
A fleeting moment, where silence sighs.
In the world's rush, we often miss,
The sacred pause, the gentle bliss.

A breath held softly, time to reflect,
In those still seconds, we reconnect.
Thoughts flutter softly, dreams take form,
In the space between, our hearts stay warm.

Echoes of laughter, whispers of love,
Filling the void, like stars above.
In silence we hear what words can't say,
In the space between, we find our way.

Rhapsody of Rest

Under the blanket of a twilight sky,
We find our place, where dreams can fly.
The lull of the night, a gentle tune,
A rhapsody of rest, beneath the moon.

Crickets sing soft, the winds caress,
In this moment, we find our rest.
The world fades away, worries cease,
Wrapped in the warmth of tranquil peace.

Stars twinkle faintly, a cosmic light,
Guiding our spirits through the night.
In dreams, we wander, in calm we nest,
Lost in the rhapsody of sweet rest.

The Vibrance of Silence

In a world that rarely stands still,
Silence bursts forth, a vibrant thrill.
Colors unseen in hushed retreat,
A canvas filled with quiet heartbeat.

The absence of noise, a symphony pure,
In silence, we feel the heart's allure.
Awakening senses, a gentle dawn,
Where thoughts unfurl and beauty is drawn.

With every breath, we paint the air,
In the vibrance of silence, we lay bare.
Finding meaning where chaos once rose,
In the stillness, our true self glows.

Currents of Calmness

In whispers soft, the waters flow,
A gentle touch, a soothing glow.
Beneath the sky, where silence reigns,
The heart finds peace, and hope remains.

Ripples grace the tranquil deep,
Where sighs of dreams and secrets sleep.
A moment held, a breath in time,
Where thoughts can dance, and spirits climb.

The world outside may roar and rush,
But here within, there's only hush.
Through currents strong, we drift and sway,
In calmness found, we find our way.

Embracing light, while shadows pass,
Our spirits soar, as waves amass.
In currents deep, we find our song,
Where hearts unite, we all belong.

Threads of Resolve and Resilience

In woven strands of will and grace,
We stitch our dreams, embrace the chase.
Through trials faced, we stand so tall,
With hearts aflame, we heed the call.

Each setback met, each tear we shed,
A testament of strength, we're led.
In bonds unbroken, we will thrive,
With every challenge, we arrive.

The fabric of our lives entwined,
In every pause, a truth we find.
We rise again, through stormy skies,
With threads of hope, our spirit flies.

Through darkened paths, we carve our way,
With every step, we light the day.
In unity, we break the chains,
Threads of resolve, where love remains.

Cradle of Contemplation

In quiet corners, thoughts take shape,
A gentle breath, a mind escape.
The world retreats, the chaos dims,
In stillness deep, our spirit swims.

A cradle soft, where dreams unfold,
The stories whispered, bright and bold.
In moments frozen, time stands still,
We weave our thoughts, we shape our will.

With every sigh, reflections bloom,
In shadows cast, we find the room.
To ponder life, to question fate,
In contemplation, we navigate.

From silence born, ideas rise,
In gentle waves, we touch the skies.
The cradle holds, as we give chase,
To every thought, it finds its place.

Shadows Dancing with Light

In twilight's grace, where shadows play,
The light ignites the dusk's ballet.
Each flicker bright, each silhouette,
In harmony, they dance, and met.

The whispers of the night unfold,
As dreams are spun, and tales are told.
With every turn, a new design,
In shadow's arms, the stars align.

A tapestry of dark and bright,
In every pulse, a spark ignites.
The rhythms swirl in twilight's embrace,
As shadows weave through time and space.

In dance of duality, we find,
That light and dark are intertwined.
In this embrace, our fears take flight,
As shadows dance with purest light.

Echoes of Tranquility

In the hush of dawn, silence sings,
Whispers of peace on gentle wings.
Nature unfolds its soft embrace,
Resting soul finds a sacred space.

Waves of calm lap at the shore,
Each heartbeat echoes, wanting more.
Beneath the trees where shadows blend,
Moments linger, yet never end.

Stars twinkle bright in the night,
A canvas of dreams bathed in light.
In this stillness, worries cease,
Breathing deeply, we find our peace.

The Dance of Stillness

In the quiet, shadows sway,
Nature's rhythm, night and day.
Leaves rustle like a soft tune,
Beneath the gaze of the pale moon.

Time drifts slowly, a gentle stream,
Thoughts linger like a fleeting dream.
In this moment, we lose our strife,
Embracing the beauty of still life.

With each breath, we find our grace,
Inward journey to a sacred place.
The heart beats in a tranquil flow,
In the dance of stillness, we grow.

Finding Balance Within

In the chaos, we seek the light,
Moments fleeting, out of sight.
Yet in silence, wisdom thrives,
   Unity within us, it strives.

The scales of life are meant to sway,
   Past and future, night and day.
Embrace the tension, find your flow,
Let inner strength and calmness grow.

Grounded in truth, we rise anew,
With every challenge, courage too.
In the heart of storms, we stand,
   Balanced gently, life in hand.

Symphony of the Heart

In every beat, a story told,
Emotions woven with threads of gold.
Harmony flows like a river wide,
Melodies carried with the tide.

Joy and sorrow, hand in hand,
Life's sweet music, a tender band.
Chords of laughter punctuate the air,
Notes of longing linger there.

Together we weave this sound divine,
Creating rhythms, yours and mine.
In the symphony, we play our part,
A masterpiece, the song of the heart.

In Search of the Quiet

In a world so loud and bright,
I seek a space of calm and light.
Where whispers dance on gentle air,
And time is free, without a care.

Amidst the noise of daily grind,
I search for peace, a treasure kind.
A moment's breath, a silent pause,
To find my thoughts, a gentle cause.

The rustle of the leaves above,
A serenade, the song of love.
In quietude, my spirit soars,
Unlocking dreams behind closed doors.

So here I roam, with heart aligned,
In solitude, my soul unbinds.
In search of quiet, I will find,
The solace deep within my mind.

Beneath the Canopy of Thought

Beneath the shade of ancient trees,
I wander through the gentle breeze.
Each thought a leaf that drifts away,
In nature's arms, I yearn to stay.

The sunlight sifts through branches high,
Illuminating dreams that fly.
In whispers soft, the secrets share,
As time unfolds its tender care.

Reflections dance upon the stream,
A tapestry of every dream.
Beneath the canopy, I'm free,
In nature's song, I find my plea.

With every step, a spark ignites,
A journey of both heart and sights.
In quiet moments, wisdom lingers,
As thoughts entwine like gentle fingers.

Threads of Peace

In the fabric of my day,
I weave the threads of peace at play.
With gentle colors, soft and bright,
I stitch my worries, day and night.

Each moment shared, a stitch of joy,
In laughter, love, nothing can destroy.
A tapestry of hearts entwined,
In harmony, our souls aligned.

Through trials faced and storms endured,
In every heartbeat, love assured.
The threads of peace, a work of art,
A masterpiece crafted from the heart.

So let me sew with tender care,
A quilt of hopes that I can share.
With every thread, my spirit flies,
A refuge found beneath the skies.

The Mosaic of My Mind

In fragments bright, my thoughts reside,
A mosaic formed with love and pride.
Each piece a memory, bold and true,
Reflecting colors of me and you.

In silent corners, shadows play,
Echoes of laughter, night and day.
The puzzle stretches, pieces blend,
In every corner, stories mend.

With every break, a chance to grow,
A dance of light, a radiant glow.
In chaos found, I take my stand,
The beauty born from heart and hand.

So here I sit, my mind a feast,
A canvas rich, my thoughts released.
The mosaic shines, a life unrolled,
In every piece, my story told.

Milton Keynes UK
Ingram Content Group UK Ltd.
UKHW022006091024
449514UK00007B/66